GUEST BOOK

Paige Tate & Co.

ISBN: 9781958803233
Printed in China

KORIE HEROLD

WWW.KORIEHEROLD.COM